THE SWAN WALLPAPER

Belinda Bradley was born in North Manchester in 1973 and now lives in Derbyshire. She has had a poem published in *Beyond the Storm*, an anthology of poems about the coronavirus. She has been a finalist in the Aesthetica Creative Writing Award and has been on the longlist for the National Poetry Competition. Belinda has had a variety of jobs including a charity shop manager, a group coordinator for the Alzheimer's Society and currently works as an occupational therapy assistant for the NHS on a mental health ward.

The Swan Wallpaper

BELINDA BRADLEY

Valley Press

First published in 2022 by Valley Press
Woodend, The Crescent, Scarborough, YO11 2PW
www.valleypressuk.com

ISBN 978-1-912436-90-3
Cat. no. VP0205

A CIP record for this book is available from the British Library.

Cover and text design by Peter Barnfather.
Edited by Jamie McGarry.

Printed and bound in Great Britain
by TJ Books Limited.

Contents

Everywhere, White

Finally, the postman delivers it,
the deer jewellery holder
I had ordered over a week ago.
I place it on my printer –

on the paper, a tree grows
out of nowhere the branches bare.
Snow has been falling for days.
Everywhere white, the sky, the air

that snakes in through the window as I sleep.
My car is losing itself on the drive
like Gretel wandering deeper into the forest.
On the fourth day I walk into town,

talk to people I haven't seen for weeks.
There are queues at the bakers,
bread is rationed, two loaves each.
At bedtime I put the holder on my locker,

adorn it with bracelets, necklaces and rings.
In the concertina moonlight
its eyes are fireflies in a jar.
The lid tightly closed.

The Red Door
for Sarah

My friend and I sit in the sunshine,
following the winter of 2013.
The winter that seemed to go on and on
like a comedian who thinks he is funny.

You show me the English rose teacup
and saucer from the local charity shop,
another one to add to your collection.
Your husband complains your house

is too small to display them all.
You were born in the wrong time,
I picture you as a 1940s housewife,
in a flared dress, your hair in rollers,

an eggless cake in the oven.
We wait for the red door to open,
the school children will pour
like dolly mixtures from a jar.

They carry cardboard sculptures,
items in an auction sale.
That day you talk about going away,
saying you don't want to leave.

I pass your house after you've gone,
listen for laughter in the back yard,
but there is none, only silence
that goes on and on.

The Swan Wallpaper

my twin sister and I had picked
to decorate our attic bedroom
had been discontinued.

Instead we settled for
a pink and white grid design.
Inadequate, like when I went

to a birthday party alone;
my twin refused to go.
At home time I closed my eyes,

rummaged through a clear bag,
pulled out a rectangular eraser
from the lucky dip.

When all I really wanted
was the doll in the matchbox.

Clay Pigeon Shooting

Something I have longed to do for real,
since playing a clay pigeon game
on a caravan holiday in Aviemore,
one Christmas when I was young.

A woman in her thirties joins us.
She has blonde bobbed hair
and wears a knitted beret,
the colour of fresh blood.

Being inquisitive I enquire why she's doing this.
Her answer, *I want to feel the power of holding a gun.*
I make a mental note to check with my husband
where our life insurance is.

The coach delivers a short briefing.
You can't take part if you're pregnant,
a couple of years back a girl found out
the morning of the shoot and had to tell
her boyfriend the news.

People experience a variety of emotions.
Some cry immediately after shooting a clay.

On his first attempt my other half gets 7 out of 7.
Thankfully, I manage to hit a few,
even though the shotgun
is nearly the same height as me.

Our fellow participant improves with each round.
At the end she gives us a hug
asks *whether we would like to go for a drink?*
We consider it briefly, then politely decline.

First Night in The Holiday Villa

I didn't mind the trains
travelling both ways, from Portugal to Spain,
speeding past pinstriped
fields of yellow and green.

In a silver frame, above my bed,
a young woman combs her copper hair.
In the background, children skate,
ghostly reflections on a frozen lake.

In the dark, the air conditioning booms;
it is a ship lost in the fog.
The fig and olive trees touch,
paper dolls facing the breeze.

Next morning, I find our son asleep
on the sofa in the lounge,
drowning in his dad's dressing gown,
sinking deeper and deeper.

The Moon

i.m. Wendy

On holiday, the moon a scuba diver's lamp
in the swimming pool.
I think of you not two months dead,

try to recall the last thing you said,
as you lifted the shopping
from the boot of your car.

A fortnight later through my window
I watch your daughters play air guitar
on a red brick wall,

aware if they fall, they will be
put back together again,
their voices canaries set free.

Outside JFK

It is 37 degrees,
the priest has disappeared
with the passport control officer.

The heat kidnaps us,
places a hand over our mouths.
Yellow taxis beep non-stop.

Our daughter flops down on a suitcase,
sprawled out like the sunflower
on her desk at home,

her window permanently locked
for fear of bees or wasps
and other winged creatures.

Longhouse in Donegal

He proposes to me as the sea
comes in on Banna beach.
I am eating a chocolate brownie
and drop it in the sand.

His parents' longhouse is white,
the sash windows pink.
There is a row of cookie jars
next to the Belfast sink, all empty.

My future mum-in-law perches
on the settee, a robin about to fly.
A lighthouse towers over the inglenook,
waves rough as a new grave.

At night, the two of us
retire to the old oak bed,
listen to the ghosts of young sailors
shipwrecked in a storm.

In the early hours of the morning
wake to hear German Shepherd dogs,
Poll and Cass, named after stars,
jumping up at the nailed-shut window.

When our daughter is born,
we cram a travel cot in a corner
of the damp guest room, the missing
shape in an abstract painting.

The three of us like to wander
among the sheep and the sweeping grass.
Five days on, we wave goodbye,
the light retreating to where it came from.

The Twins

We do everything together, speak our own language
that nobody understands. Teachers make us sit
in the same seat each lesson; often we swop.

I catch the measles first, then give it my sister
not wanting her to feel left out. Our rash spreads,
head to toe, a dot-to-dot puzzle in a Christmas annual.

I recover after a week but she's admitted to hospital,
struggling to breathe. I draw spots on her doll's face,
convinced they will go away when she gets better.

Now there is only me, teachers know who I am.
Black ink is poisoning my sister's doll,
damp rising in an abandoned house.

The Replacement Bear

When she gets home from school,
she is summoned to the front room.
Mother has Walter by his legs,
dangling him over the open fire.
The fur on his head glows,
a row of exclamation marks.

Someone is screaming far off,
at the bottom of a disused well.
Pine needles drop from her eyes,
a forest is born with birds,
wildflowers and a fawn hiding
in the shadows.

Her father rips him apart,
throws his limbs into the fire.
The flames reach higher.
They offer her a new bear,
a bow around its neck,
which she refuses to accept.

Haliburton Forest

I wouldn't have gone if I had known
there would be bears.
It doesn't help that our chalet
is called *The Bear's Den*.

And to make matters worse,
there's a large rip in one of the sofas,
the other a dip
as if a road has collapsed.

The room is packed for the wolf talk.
When it's over we all go
to the edge of the forest,
our torches showing us the way.

The presenter kneels
on the tarmac path,
hands covering his mouth
in the shape of a single flame.

His howl is a black tent
unzipping the sky.
A silence from the crowd
like falling snow.

We hear cries haunting
as the voices of the dead,
stale bread sticks
in people's throats.

Dear Tree

Dear Tree on the Banks of the River Taw,

Thanks for saving my life last week. One minute I was walking on dry land, the next I was in water waist-deep and rising. I managed to haul myself up onto the roof of a car, but slipped and was swept away. You came along and I hung onto your trunk for nearly an hour, sleep a cold caller knocking. I am not religious but I prayed, promised whoever was listening I will change. I admit I've been a shit dad. Yesterday I took my nine-year-old son to his first football match, our team won 2-1.

Dear Apple Blossom,

Often I forget, pour two cups of tea, expect to see her dozing in the leather armchair or hear her footsteps on the stairs. We were together forty-eight years, met on the last bus home. She said she liked men with beards. I open the living room curtains, see you in full bloom; it reminds me of my wife on our wedding day.

Dear Maple,

Just wanted to say thank you for letting my boyfriend climb you to enter my bedroom. It can't have been very pleasant as he's seventeen stone and has big feet. He's a keen rugby player. I am pleased to announce that I'm pregnant. Which I am happy about, although mum went mad when she found out, can't blame her really as I'm fifteen. The scan showed a girl. We're going to name her Maple, after you.

Dear Pine,

You and me have something in common; we are both tall. I have a medical condition which is why I am tall. At school I was teased, called *the leaning tower of Lisa.* Three years ago I was shopping in Camden Town and got approached by a model scout. Since then I have travelled all the world, New York, Paris, Madrid, Mexico. Tomorrow I'm off to Chicago; can't wait, I'm so excited.

Dear Oak,

When I'm with you I'm not scared of anything: spiders, clowns, the buzzing sound in my ear, thunderstorms, nuclear war or Lucifer, the cat next door. When I'm with you I'm not scared of the dark, Morgan Moonscar from Scooby Doo, balloons with smiley faces on or mummy's friend when he's had a few. When I'm with you flying on my homemade swing I'm not scared of anything.

Baby Grows Up with Peter Rabbit

and just before ten, Friday night, is driven home
by a mum of a boy I do not know, drunk unable
to stand, mobile phone clutched in his hand.

I apologise on my son's behalf,
relieved he hasn't thrown up in her car.
We adapt a figure of four hold to stop him

falling flat on his face, although it seems
like he already has as there is grass
on his lips and in his hair.

I assist him up the stairs, his shoes leave
muddy prints enroute like he's been
on a bear hunt with friends.

He manages to tell me he's had a third of
a bottle of gin, probably pink, judging by
the liquid in the washing up bowl.

My partner hugs him as he moans, he's all arms
and legs like the Worzel Gummidge puppet
I once owned and rarely took out the box.

We decide not to visit A & E, put him
in the recovery position, take it in turns
to sit by his bed, every now and then

check his breathing is normal and
his skin isn't pale or has a blue tinge.
I do the graveyard shift.

As the streetlamps switch off one by one,
like fifteen candles on a birthday cake,
I pinch myself to stay awake.

Dylan's Candy Bar – New York

My son chooses the ones which leave a fizz
on your tongue like trapped bubbles.

He squishes the sweets into a clear paint can:
Neon Gummy Worms, Sour Patch Kids,

Granny Smith Apple Bears. He has nearly run
out of space when water makes its way

under the door, rushes down the stairs
as if a school is breaking up for summer.

In our hotel room on the 23rd floor,
the four of us watch an invisible corn broom

sweeping across the Hudson river. Lightning hits
the water towers shaped like circus tents,

the rain smudges everything in its path,
a left-handed arm on a charcoal drawing.

The School Trip

We leave before the coach comes.
Now he's twelve
he doesn't want us to stay.

I open his door, blue walls
and a blue floor. I lie on his bed,
adrift in the middle of the sea.

I think of him, headphones on,
travelling through France, Belgium
and the Netherlands.

While others sleep, his hand
in his rucksack,
feeling the dark for sweets.

The Birthday Party

After the party
I didn't sleep well,
remembering the girl in the shower,
fully-clothed, unexpected

as an owl flying in daylight
through a parting in a wood.
Do you want me to open the door? I ask.
I can do that myself, she says,

stepping onto a snow-white rug
in red glitter shoes.
Later, she locks herself
in one of the bedrooms,

her shadow falls across
a black cat sleeping
on a sunlit windowsill;
claws reach out, ready to kill.

To Abbie

Imagine if we could start all over again,
you and Hannah sitting on the bench
in front of a post office

that is no longer a post office
and me approaching not knowing
what to expect.

It's my first day of a new job
after a long break. The date,
November the thirteenth,

not a Friday although it might well
have been. The sky is pale
as a child lost in the snow.

We wait for our lift,
time passing like a dog walking
with a poorly leg.

At head office, induction:
*write down something exciting
about yourself.*

A colleague does taxidermy
(brave to admit, considering
our employer is an animal charity).

There are two squirrels, a vole and
a bat in her freezer. She carries
a pair of plastic gloves, just in case.

In teams we dress a mannequin,
rummage through a mountain
of women's clothes and shoes,

determined to win.
Since leaving, I recall the shop,
the steep steps into the cellar,

the cave at the back,
the stone bench,
the sense of being watched.

My Last Day at Carsington Water

Before I start work, I sit in the car,
sunlight dances on the reservoir,
sending message in Morse code.

When customers enter the shop,
it's the name of their dogs
I find most interesting,

Sherlock, Winston, Hetty.
Images surface like dead fish:
a pipe, a bow tie, an elderly aunt,

that used to knit us siblings
a jumper every Christmas,
the cuffs and collars always too small,

the wool itching our skin.
In colours we would never wear:
violet, peppermint or lavender.

At six pm, there's a howling wind.
I gather in the goods from outside,
flip the notice, *Sorry We Are Closed*.

Refuse to look back.

Truly Fair

I want to be a dog, like my sister;
wear a white and grey coat, a sample
from Aunt Mabel's clothing shop.
Fake fur soft as my pink pencil case,
that I can't help but stroke in class.

She wears a dog mask, eyes oval-shaped
like the mahogany mirror in our hall.
A silver chain in one hand,
as if taking herself for a walk.

My job is to unpack a wicker basket
onto a red and black tartan rug.
No lines to be said or woofs to be barked,
no special costume needed.

The day after the play, in maths,
my fountain pen leaks,
bleeds into a corner of my pencil case,
leaving a dark patch,
a crow with a broken wing.

The Tavern

I choose the wooden seat,
having a thing for benches,

especially the pew type.
My daughter is opposite me,

three months off fifteen,
I don't often see her up close.

She is the unfinished sketch
of a girl on her desk,

her ambition to be an astrophysicist.
There is no let-up in the wind

coming from the Atlantic
as we make our way back to the car.

The driver's seat has a dusting
of gold glitter from a dress I wore

for a Christmas party, as if all the stars
have plummeted from the sky.

Holiday in the Black Forest

The Braeburns didn't survive the journey
to Hofsgrund. They turned soft on the inside
like imperial mints.

I feed them to the horses, Tristen and Moritz,
my hand flat as if I'm about to receive the cane,
juice and pips escape from their mouths.

During a storm, on the fourth day, a shadow
of a horse's head flashes up on the stable wall.
His body a JCB digging the foundations.

On the ferry home from Rotterdam to Hull
our daughter finishes off her art homework
on the top bunk. She is colouring in an apple,

making the flesh go bad. As night falls,
through the porthole, beams of light
punctuate the dark.

The Desk Tidy

I send the elephant back in a box, courtesy of Hermes.
It came broken, one tab missing.

The next week, its replacement: not a like for like
but heavier, made from one piece.

I put it on my pedestal desk. The desk I'd planned
to paint in the summer. It retains a look of distress,

like my face when my daughter's high school phones
to say she's not showed up.

I leave work, drive past the Knockerdown pub
and the flood sign, images flashing through my mind

like a person's life when their parachute fails to open.
Approximately a mile from home, I receive a text;

everything is fine. The office hadn't got
all the registers, it was mock exam time.

In the evening, the elephant watches over me
as I write, its eye a black moon in a copper sky.

The Invincibles

When school has finished,
a fortnight before the Easter break,
a group of year elevens
hike up to the StarDisc
with supplies of beer and crisps.
They step over the flattened
barbed wire fence
and stand near the edge.
The day is fine but cold.
These pupils will be known
as the GCSE-cancelled generation.
They are the *Invincibles*
not at risk from the coronavirus,
or so they think.

This chapter they will carry
close to their chest like a war token.
They will bring it out at birthday parties
as if it's a magic trick,
tell their children and grandchildren,
until they're sick of hearing about it.
And fifty years from now
answer questions on the news:
how did they feel when it happened?
Did they get the exam grades they'd expected?
Did it change their perspective on life?

My daughter used to stay up late to revise,
the light moving under her door
like a keyboard being played.
After the prime minister's announcement
I can see the disbelief on her face
like a portrait falling in an earthquake.
I offer my condolences,
reassure her everything will be okay.

Anthony Gell School

Quarter to nine, the high school bell rings;
there's no one about, only myself and
a paperboy finishing his round.
Bears gaze out of front windows,
mournful expressions on their faces,
remembering life before lockdown.
After lunch, an ice cream van blasts a slow
version of Greensleeves like a soundtrack
from a horror movie. I search the streets
but it's nowhere to be seen.

Mother's Day in the Time of the Coronavirus

I am not allowed to visit my mother.
I send her an Amazon gift voucher

so she can buy some books,
as all the libraries have closed.

When I was ten years old, I ordered
a rose for Mother's Day from Avon,

the glass petals filled with perfume.
It was smaller than it looked

in the glossy catalogue.
Around five o'clock my daughter

gives me a Mother's Day card,
hand drawn by herself,

a blue butterfly hovers over
a dandelion, reluctant to move on.

Buying a Second-hand Bike off eBay

She rides down Chapel Lane,
her light brown hair free

to do as it pleases.
This could be a scene from a film set,

the soft-focus effect,
a sheet of tracing paper

attached to a lens.
Cherry blossom falls

at just the right speed
and the shadows

are perfectly placed.
The frame the colour of tangerines,

which she hasn't eaten for years.
Our teenage daughter disappears –

we wait in silence for her
to come back to us.

Grey

A herd of elephants hang in the sky
and I recall the story of a paraglider
who during a storm got lost in a cloud.
She survived despite falling unconscious
and having to cope with frostbite.
Outside the shop I put a face covering on
for the first time; it is difficult to breathe,
the humidity not helping. I think back
to the beginning, my husband ambling
into the kitchen, a pair of grey underpants
that used to be white as a mask.
How we all laughed and I joked with him
saying *I hope they are clean.*

Fox Clouds

Enid is alone in the house she and her two
sisters grew up in, never left. She has a budgie
for company, Joey, named after their dad.
It appeared on the doorstep, the evening
of his death, like a teaspoon of sunshine.

At night, she's certain she can hear her
older sister's breaths through the paper-skin
walls, delicate as the wings of a moth.
On cloud-free days, she hangs her washing
on the line, watched by the gnomes,

the name of the shed, *Fox Clouds*, chosen by
their mother, barely visible. Often, she sees
her younger sister in the Queen Anne chair
next to the picture window, her hair
in pigtails as if she's a little girl again.

The Hills

It's the not knowing,
the not knowing where he is,
on a good-to-be-alive day like this.
The sun throws down its parachute of warmth.

He vanished before the dawn chorus.
She can still hear the front door
slamming shut like a piano lid
onto someone's fingers.

Why did she ask him to marry her?
It wasn't even a leap year.
Home is a stethoscope
listening for a heartbeat.

She takes out her wedding dress,
cuts it into bits: a blizzard.
She is alone on these hills,
the cold curtains of rain opening and closing.

GCSE Results Day 2020

My daughter takes out the slip of paper
from the manila envelope;
it looks fragile, like it can rip easily
if handled incorrectly.

I lead her into the conservatory
that we never use,
with views of sheep moving like clouds.
The sky seems bright.

On the Persian rug is a cardboard box,
big enough to fit a human; she opens it,
a bouquet of gold balloons emerges,
a phoenix flapping from the ashes.

Tittesworth Reservoir

The rain is a ballerina *en pointe*; circles
and circles form on the reservoir,
like Venn diagrams overlapping.

The rain becomes an onslaught of arrows
attacking us and the kayaks.
I mourn our lost holiday to Umbria,

to the castle crossed off on today's date.
The changing rooms are closed,
we peel off our clothes in a marquee,

epidermises from white onions.
Back home, I line up our trainers
in the sunshine to dry,

like soldiers on parade.
I realise one of my son's shoes
is a size smaller than the other.

The Future

My husband and I consider the future,
after the vaccine when we no longer need
to social distance or wear a mask.

I ask my son where he would like to go
when this is over. He says *Budapest*
because of the architecture.

I find a holiday apartment on the internet,
an empty bird cage in the living room,
floor-to-ceiling windows shaped

like fake fingernails.
I want to stay there, take in light
until it overwhelms me

and stand on the balcony,
hold out my arm like Snow White,
entice the birds to come.

Rain

It is raining,
rain that doesn't hold back.
It staggers sideways and I fight to remain upright.

The wind in the tunnel is harsh.
Cumbrians say it is so strong, you can see it coming,
but I hadn't seen it coming.

I hadn't seen the walls closing in like the shiny bars
of the electric machine used to measure my feet
when I was small.

In the Slate Mine café, I try to ignore
the noises in my head as if the quarrymen
are hammering deep underground.

I would love to stay, watch the rain
fall through the picture window,
study its angle of descent.

In my halls of residence, an A4 notepad
waits patiently, power lines in a white sky,
anticipating the arrival of the birds.

A Game of Monopoly

Yesterday the sun became red,
Sahara dust from Hurricane Ophelia,
and he gave me the boot as if
we were playing a game of Monopoly.

He said we were going round in circles.
I think of Jane Eyre and her friend
in the rain, wearing placards; Rebellion
and Vain, a flat iron in each hand.

In our set the iron
has been replaced by a cat;
cats are much more trustworthy.
I wonder who my replacement is?

Six months on, I rummage through his stuff,
that he hasn't bothered picking up;
discover his old Monopoly set, the one
he played with as a child.

I take out the racing car,
throw it onto the open fireplace,
it goes up in flames; I am
amazed at how quickly it burns.

Mascot

If he had asked me do I want to have a go
after watching the quad biking safety video
I would have said no.

A and E is a goldfish bowl with too many fish
Everyone is wearing a blue mask,
I attempt to open a Kit-Kat one handed.

That night I sleep on my back,
my left arm in a cast
like a lucky cat waving.

The Forest of Bowland

I don't do camping but this is glamping;
a flushing toilet, no running hot water
but a wood-fired stove, deep mattresses
with Egyptian cotton sheets. It is cold
for early September. The safari tent has its
mouth wide open, a whale eager to swallow
us up. A silhouette of a cow is tied to a pole,
social distance 1 metre written below. There is
no way I am getting within one metre of a cow.

I like rustic, but the dining table is taking it too
far; in the wood are huge gaps as though it has
been attacked by an axe, two black candle
chandeliers hang above. I trick my mind into
believing the traffic from the M6 is the wind.
I can live without traffic noise but I cannot live
without the wind. During the next couple of days,
I travel back in time, crave light like an ex-smoker
desperate for a cigarette.

Elvaston Castle Country Park

There is no escaping the mud;
it is everywhere,
a mutant virus spreading across the globe.

Our daughter remembered the Redwoods,
tells us they are native to California.
One towers above our heads like a rocket.

The sun briefly shows its face,
a child peeping out from behind a tree,
the bark glows like a flame.

Entry to the *Old English garden*
is through a wrought iron gate,
we follow the one-way system.

The place is desolate
but there are signs of life,
daffodil shoots, liliums,

and a shrub called
Young Lady
not fully developed.

At the Garden Centre

I shelter under a canopy.
Around the corner our daughter
chooses some strawberry plants.
I had wanted to call her April
but she was born in June.
In the cubicle next to me,
a baby screamed non-stop
like a mating fox.
The wind becomes stronger,
creating a new path.
She finally decides
on Honeye and Elsanta.
I can't eat hairy fruits
such as strawberries or kiwis.
When I was on holiday in Greece,
I drank a bright green cocktail
at a club, my throat burned,
sharp as a barbed wire fence.
That night in our poky apartment
the walls moved like the rabbit jelly
mum used to carry
on a leaf-patterned plate
to the dining table.
I would fight with my sister
for the bushy tail.
My friend slept through
the earthquake.

The Lodge

After dark, while everyone is asleep,
the mischief of mice scale the base cabinets,
admire their reflections in the black rock,
nibble the cake I had saved from the surf shop
at Coldingham Bay; white foam on the top and
hundreds of dots like a painting in an art gallery,
stand at a distance to decipher the meaning.
They leave a hole in the sponge,
a crater on Saturn's moon.

Leaving our Teenagers Alone Overnight
for the First Time

It felt as though we were taking a risk.
Walking along the corridor, facemasks on,
the emerald carpet like the robe
of a princess faded by the sun.

The hotel room itself looked normal.
There was still soap, shampoo, conditioner
in tiny bottles, a packet of ginger biscuits
and those hard-to-open milk pots.

In the evening I phoned home
but there was no mobile reception.
My son's recorded voice echoed
back at me before the line went dead.

From the enormous window
I could see the hills of Dovedale,
bold and unafraid. A grey and white cow
was munching so close

I could almost touch it.
I could hear the grass
being pulled from the ground,
surprised at how loud it sounded.

The Morning after Halloween

there are witches' broomsticks scattered
all over the park and chicken's feet.
The rain is the kind of rain I hate,

neither strong or weak.
Gucci and Prada are gone,
along with two hundred cats

from our town in the past eight months.
I am not a fan of labels,
mine are from a rescue place,

alphabetically named after handbags.
The trees reach out their arms,
offering me comfort

but there is none to be had.
The sky darkens like a mirror,
turning black around the edges.

Royal Derby Hospital

I walk past the badgers in the courtyard,
overawed to see the creatures in the light.
They have survived storm after storm,
too many to name them all. There are three,

larger than life, constructed from brown and
white willow, in various poses as if modelling
for a shoot. It's the one standing I like the best,
an adult perhaps? I want to touch its nose,

reach up and stroke its forehead,
feel the wood brush against my hand.
But there is a sheet of glass
between us, a mask.

Autumn

Despite the weather forecast I wear a dress
with red and navy flowers.
From a distance it can be mistaken
for wallpaper or a bed spread.

Autumn is an unwanted visitor
appearing overnight
as my mother-in-law did,
her life packed into a set of suitcases.

When I get back from taking my car
for its M.O.T. the teenagers are still asleep.
They will rise between one and three
like anchors raised from the seabed.

The dog lies in a ladder of sunlight
next to the new fireplace.
There is a space above,
waiting to be filled.

I plan to buy a porthole mirror,
so I can pretend I am watching
a seagull fly above a deck,
losing itself in the falling dark.

Oxford

Magdalen College

My husband asks,
are you going to take any photographs?
I said no, not wanting to experience the place
through a screen – and even if I had,
the images hardly ever turn out the way
you'd planned. The gargoyles never in focus,
the long corridors lacking atmosphere,
a supernatural film without any shadows.
There were no ducks in the duckery,
although there were deer in the deer park.
On the riverside terrace the leaves fall
from the trees without any warning.

Christchurch College – The Great Hall

I could eat breakfast here every day,
feel the weight of the portraits:
the writers, politicians, kings and
queens, bearing down on me.

I could choose from the mini cereal boxes
on display, bigger than the ones I recall
from my childhood, on rare occasions
we stayed in hotels.

I always wanted more.

Lockdown Number 3

It should be light by now
but it feels like the middle of the night.
It's minus three, the fog a murmuration
of starlings, making it hard to see.
Salt rainbows form on my car windscreen,
I wipe them away but they keep coming back.

This Morning is on in the hospital waiting room.
Dr Chris Steele tells us to put things into perspective.
There have been over a thousand deaths in the past
24 hours, equivalent to three jumbo jets
crashing daily and all the passengers dying.

In the evening I apply online for a new job,
the form asks *do you have any holidays
booked in the next three months?*

Omicron

The streets around Pinxton village hall have never been
this busy. Inside our teenage son waits for his second jab.

Just when life seems to be getting back to normal,
a new variant is identified, early data suggests its

highly contagious, the number of mutations *horrific*.
The government makes facemasks mandatory again

in shops and on public transport. The world holds its
breath once more like a passer-by playing dead during

a random shooting. We are left in the dark as though
storm Arwen has switched all the lights off.

Three weeks until Christmas. The car is a cradle rocking
in the bitter wind.

Pullman Hotel – Liverpool

We arrive during storm Dudley,
the view from the panoramic window bleak;
all we can see is mist.

When it clears the Liver birds appear
like they have flown there by magic.
I take photographs at various intervals over

the next two days, always the same shot;
the Ferris wheel to the right,
the Liver building behind.

The sky ever-changing, lifeless grey
to moody blue to sunshine white. The weather
a scrap of paper, drawn out of a hat.

Soon self-isolation will come to an end,
cases and deaths are falling. The government's plan
for *living with Covid.*

I remember the first wave, hearing a cough
from our younger son. My husband and I glancing
at each other, fear on our faces.

Cathy at The Cavern Club

I have forgotten how good live music is.
I didn't like large crowds even pre-Covid
but this is okay, the tables spaced out.

My dad wouldn't allow the band *Beer for Breakfast*
at my wedding reception. He had the final say
as he was paying. I don't drink beer only wine.

Cathy asks for requests; normally I'd look away,
like I have gone back to the classroom
and a teacher needs a volunteer to read.

But today I shout *Hey Jude*. Her gravelly
voice makes me retreat into myself as though
I am walking into the sea fully clothed.

Alarm

I wake up to *every cloud has a silver lining,*
spot a bunny-shaped one, ears pricked
as if it has heard something important.
Two years since the first lockdown occurred,
two weeks before the Easter break,
Covid has spread like wildfires
caused by fragments of broken glass.
Omicron has a new variant, BA.2,
the old one, still around.
I contemplate joining,
The Cloud Appreciation Society,
receive a free cloud daily,
emailed to my inbox.

Confessions and Reflections of an OTA
(Occupational Therapy Assistant)

The Ward

There are eighteen single,
ensuite rooms on the ward,
separated into female and male.
Each has a different-coloured door.
There is no number thirteen.

Drawing

I invite the patient to join me
in the activity room,
it's just us two as big groups
make her nervous.
She draws a cat in black felt tip,
it looks scared, fur standing on end.
She writes next to the picture,
we decided it was their time to sleep
in peace and kidney infection.

Painting

The patient has got the texture and shading
perfect, the prickliness of the spikes,
the reflection in its eye and on the surface
of its nose. Then he adds twigs and leaves,
collected from the grounds, layer upon layer
until the hedgehog goes into hibernation.

Collage

During the session a pair of navy scissors
went missing. I had counted six.
I found them hidden in a magazine.
Then later another pair went missing,
yellow this time. They failed to materialise.
After the session had finished each
of the participants' rooms was searched
by a nursing assistant. I stayed behind
to fill in an incident report form.
The next morning the scissors turned up
in the top right pocket of my white tunic.

Tangrams

From seven shapes that make a square
you can create countless puzzles,
such as a rabbit, shoe or elephant.

The physicist picks a candle,
the one who is timid a fox,
the patient who believes in
reincarnation, a butterfly.

I choose a person praying,
dress them in coral pink against
a background of seal grey.

Knit and Natter

I can do the natter but not the knit.

A patient wants to knit
a matinee jacket.
I fetch some needles
and a ball of peppermint wool.
She wraps her incontinence pad
in a towel, says *this is my baby*.
She will not give it away.

This Way to the Beach

I don't love you anymore,
his voice a dead badger
in the middle of the road.
She had known it for some time,
buried it like a pea
underneath a pile of mattresses.

Every morning, after he left,
she would sit on the window seat,
knees up, her head a sun touching
the tops of the sand dunes.
She would listen for his car,
alert as a wild bird.

This way to the beach,
as if it can be any other.
She doesn't notice it at first,
the grey on grey,
like one of those paintings
they call art.

A seal is lying on its side,
not far from the sea,
eyes pools of polished jet.
She wants to dive in,
swim to the bottom,
never come up for air.

Still Life

I choose the girl with no face
from an array of objects:
a sparkling silver moon,
a pair of ballet shoes,
a Harlequin mask,
a black rose in a cut-glass decanter.

I position around her feet,
a gold leaf bracelet
like a fallen-down crown.
Her white dress is a painted wall
overlooking the sea.

She holds a book open,
a swallow in flight.
I imagine its light grey shadow
heading south
over the wide mouth of the table.

Acknowledgements

Special thanks to Judy, without her support this book would never have been written.